www.two-canpublishing.com

Published by Two-Can Publishing,
43-45 Dorset Street, London W1U 7NA

Copyright © 2002, 1995 Two-Can Publishing

For information on Two-Can books and multimedia,
call (0)20 7224 2440, fax (0)20 7224 7005, or visit our website
at http://www.two-canpublishing.com

Text: Sue Hook, Angela Royston
Consultant: Keith Lye BA Hons. (Bristol); FRGS
Maps: Contour Publishing
Computer illustrations: Mel Pickering
Watercolour illustrations: Lindy Norton
Photo research: Liz Eddison
Editorial Directors: Sue Hook, Carolyn Jackson
Art Director: Belinda Webster
Production Director: Lorraine Estelle
Assistant Editors: Mimi George, Samantha Hilton, Deborah Kespert
Co-edition Editors: Matthew Birch, Robert Sved
Text Contributor: Karen Burns Kellaher

'Two-Can' is a trademark of Two-Can Publishing.
Two-Can Publishing is a division of Zenith Entertainment Ltd,
43-45 Dorset Street, London W1U 7NA

HB ISBN 1-85434-345-9
PB ISBN 1-84301-024-0

HB 2 3 4 5 6 7 8 9 10 05 04 03 02
PB 1 2 3 4 5 6 7 8 9 10 05 04 03 02

A catalogue record for this book is available from the British Library.

Photo credits: Robert Aberman/ The Hutchinson Library: p55; Brian and Cherry Alexander: p16, p17 (top); Tom Ang/ Robert Harding: p41 (top);
Gary Bell/ Planet Earth Pictures: p83; R I M Campbell/ Bruce Coleman: p44; John Cancalosi/ Bruce Coleman: p84 (bottom); Alain Compost/
Bruce Coleman: p79 (top); G&P Corrigan/ Robert Harding: p68 (top); Rob Cousins/ Robert Harding: p34 (bottom); Tim Defrisco/ Allsport:
p19 (bottom); Bernd Ducke/ Britstock-IFA: p61; John Egan/ The Hutchinson Library: p72; Everts/ Britstock-IFA: p50; Financial Times/ Robert
Harding: p66; JG Fuller/ The Hutchinson Library: p30; Francisco Futil/ Bruce Coleman: p67 (top); Ron Gilling/ Panos Pictures: p40; Laurent
Giradou/ Robert Harding: p33 (bottom); Grafenhain/ Britstock-IFA: p51 (top), p54; Z Harasym/ Trip: p57; Jeremy Hartley/ Panos Pictures: p40;
D&J Heaton/ Spectrum Colour Library: p79 (bottom); Jay/ Britstock-IFA: p62; M Jenkin/ Trip: p60; A A Johnson/ Spectrum Colour Library: p43;
Alexander Kuznetsov/ Trip: p63 (bottom); David Lomax/ Robert Harding: p67 (bottom); L C Marigo/ Bruce Coleman: p32 (left); New Zealand
Consulate: p84 (top); Mark Newman/ FLPA: p63 (top); S Pern/ The Hutchinson Library: p36; Pictor International: p37, p74 (top), p74 (bottom);
Picturepoint: p34 (top), p73 (top); Pictures Colour Library: p19 (top), p41 (bottom), p47 (top), p53; Dr Eckart Pott/ Bruce Coleman:
p51 (bottom); Hans Reinhard/ Bruce Coleman: p82 (top); Geoff Renner/ Robert Harding: p24; Sean Sprague/ Panos Pictures: p35;
Tony Stone Associates: p18, p22 (top), p27 (top), p27 (bottom), p33 (top), p52 (top), p52 (bottom), p68 (bottom); Telegraph Colour Library:
p26, p42, p73 (bottom); Trip: p75 (bottom); Penny Tweedie/ Panos Pictures: p82 (bottom); Philip Wolmuth/ Panos Pictures: p31 (top);
Adam Woolfitt/ Robert Harding: p25 (top), p85; ZEFA: p17 (bottom), p22 (bottom), p23 (top), p23 (bottom), p25 (bottom), p31 (bottom),
p32 (right), p45, p47 (bottom), p69, p75 (top), p87

Printed by Wing King Tong in Hong Kong

A First Atlas

How to use this book

Look it up!
An atlas is designed to help you look for information about the many places in the world. This one is organized by geographical regions. You can find them listed on the Contents page.

Pronunciation
Some words, such as encyclopedia (say "en-sy-clo-pee-dee-a"), are difficult to pronounce. To say them correctly, make the sounds in the brackets after each of the words.

Cross-references
Above the coloured bar on each map there is a list of entries in the other three books in the *Scholastic First Encyclopedia*, with their book titles. These entries tell you more about the subject on the page.

Contents
The Contents page at the front of the book lists the main entries, or subjects in the book, and which page they are on.

Glossary
Words in the book that may be difficult to understand are marked in **bold**. The Glossary near the back of the book lists these words and explains what they mean.

Index
The Index at the back of the book is a list of everything mentioned in the book, arranged in alphabetical order, with its page number. If an entry is in *italics*, it means that it is a label on a map. If the page number only is in *italics*, the entry appears in the main text as well as being a map label.

Contents

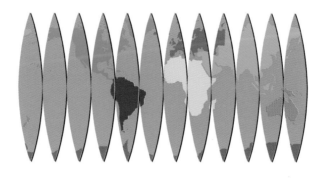

The Earth

The Earth is a huge ball floating in space. Scientists believe that more than 4,500 million years ago it was a tiny speck of dust in a cloud of gas that formed our Sun and solar system. The Earth became at first a ball of super-hot liquid material. During millions of years a thin layer of lava and rock cooled and hardened. This became the Earth's crust. The crust has cracks, called faults, in it. Sudden movements of the crust cause **volcanic eruptions** and **earthquakes** near the faults.

Drifting continents

The world's continents rest on huge pieces of the Earth's crust, called plates.

continent of South America

overlapping plates

mantle

The plates float like rafts on the super-hot, liquid mantle beneath.

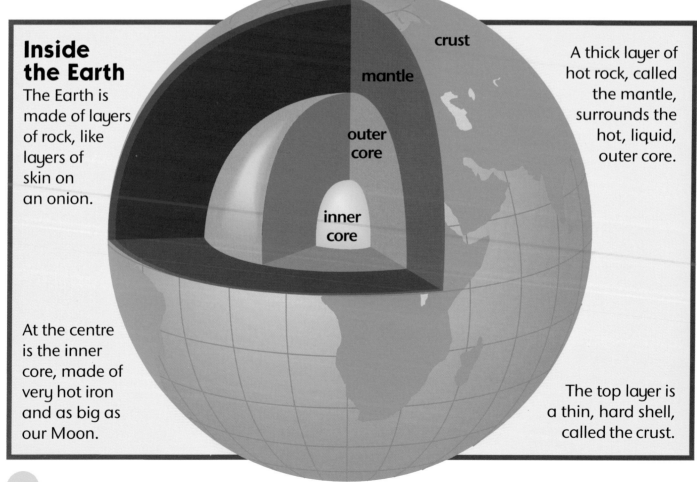

Inside the Earth

The Earth is made of layers of rock, like layers of skin on an onion.

crust

mantle

outer core

inner core

A thick layer of hot rock, called the mantle, surrounds the hot, liquid, outer core.

At the centre is the inner core, made of very hot iron and as big as our Moon.

The top layer is a thin, hard shell, called the crust.

Ancient Earth

Scientists believe that the seven continents that make up our world today were once joined together. They formed a huge jigsaw of land, which was the super-continent Pangaea (say "Pan-jay-uh").

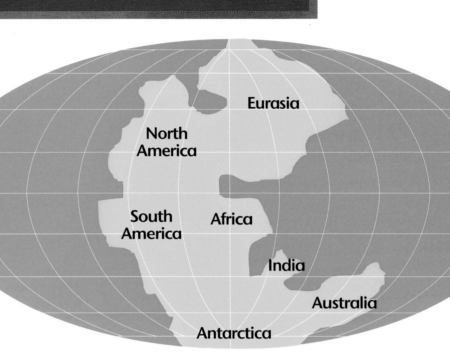

Eurasia

North America

South America

Africa

India

Australia

Antarctica

▲ The Earth (Pangaea) 200 million years ago

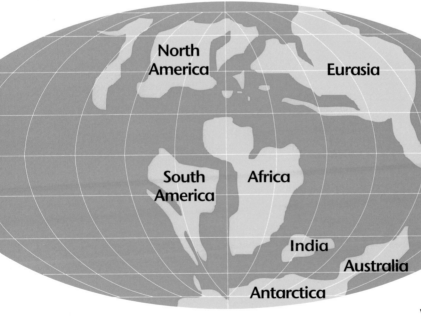

North America

Eurasia

South America

Africa

India

Australia

Antarctica

▲ The Earth 100 million years ago

Very slowly, Pangaea broke into pieces, which moved apart. Each piece became a continent. Look at the map of the world on the next page. You will see that the east coast of South America could easily fit onto the west coast of Africa, just like the pieces in a puzzle.

Maps and mapmakers

A First Atlas is a book of maps of our world. Maps are flat pictures of the Earth. The maps in this book show you the shapes of the Earth's land, oceans and seas, and where they are. Maps also show you where the hot and cold places are in the world.

Making maps

The Earth is round, like a ball, but maps are flat. Try peeling an orange, keeping the skin in one piece. Now try to lay the skin flat on a table. To make it flat, you have to squash some pieces and stretch others. This is similar to what mapmakers must do to draw maps of the Earth.

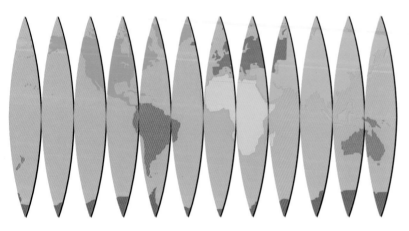

▲ This is how the Earth would look if it were laid out flat. There are big gaps at the top and bottom.

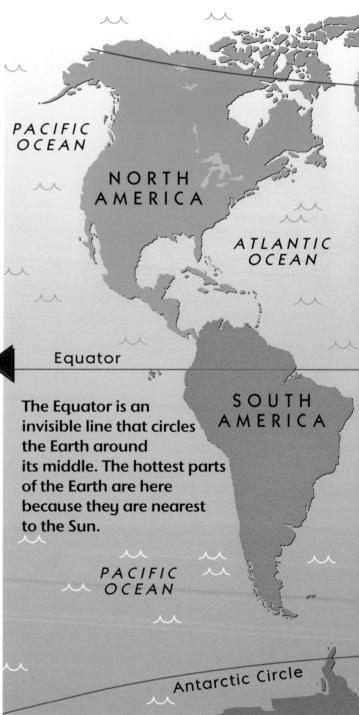

The Equator is an invisible line that circles the Earth around its middle. The hottest parts of the Earth are here because they are nearest to the Sun.

Four big oceans and many seas cover about two thirds of the Earth. You can find the names of the oceans on the map of the world.

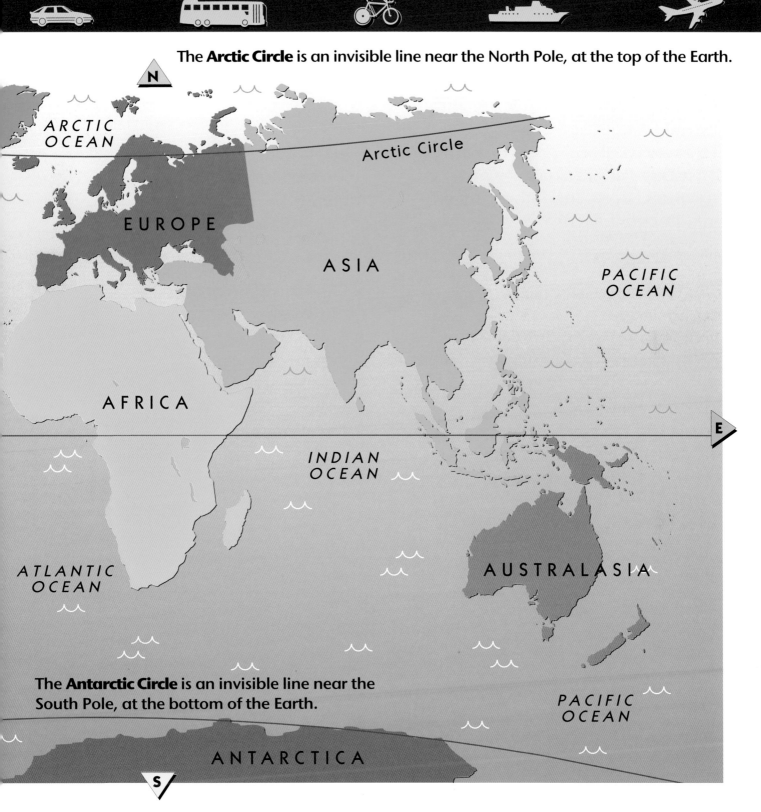

The **Arctic Circle** is an invisible line near the North Pole, at the top of the Earth.

N

ARCTIC OCEAN

Arctic Circle

EUROPE

ASIA

PACIFIC OCEAN

AFRICA

INDIAN OCEAN

E

ATLANTIC OCEAN

AUSTRALASIA

The **Antarctic Circle** is an invisible line near the South Pole, at the bottom of the Earth.

PACIFIC OCEAN

ANTARCTICA

S

Land that is not covered by water is divided into huge areas called continents. You can see the seven continents on the map.

The Earth's continents are divided into countries. Today, there are 192 countries. Each has its own people, flag and customs.

Looking at maps

To show us places and landforms on maps, mapmakers use picture **symbols**, signs, labels and lines in different colours.

They are like a code that we need to understand in order to read the maps.

Labels

Labels tell you names of places on maps. Here are the kinds of things labelled in this atlas.

ocean	*INDIAN OCEAN*
sea	Arabian Sea
island	*Sumatra*
country	**JAPAN**
desert	Sahara Desert
forest	*Amazon Rainforest*
mountains	**Rocky Mountains**
river	Mississippi River
lake	Lake Michigan
capital city	☆ **London**
city	**Los Angeles**

The meaning of lines

Mapmakers draw some lines on maps to show where countries begin and end. These lines are called borders. They do not exist on the land; they only exist on the maps.

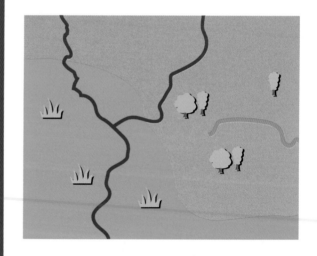

Red lines show the borders between countries.

Land signs
Picture symbols show you different kinds of land on maps.

grassland
There are grass-covered lands all over the world. Sometimes they are called savannah or pampas. Grassland is the best land for farming.

desert
Desert areas have almost no rain. Most deserts are hot and dry in the day, but cold at night. Fewer animals and plants survive here than in most other landforms.

deciduous
Deciduous trees, such as beech, birch and oak, lose their leaves in the autumn. Deciduous forests grow in cool areas.

tundra
Tundra is cold, bare **plain** near the Arctic Circle. The surface of the ground is frozen all year so the growing season is very short.

ice and snow
Thick ice covers the areas around the North and South Poles, and big storms bring snow and strong winds.

rainforest
Most rainforests grow in tropical areas near the Equator, where it is hot and wet. Rainforests are home to millions of different plants and animals.

evergreen forest
Evergreen trees such as pine, fir, spruce and larch stay green all year round. Evergreen forests grow mostly in cold areas.

mountains
Many areas of the world are covered in high, rocky mountains. Very high mountains are covered in snow.

Where are you going next?
On each map, the little red aeroplane points the way to the next **region** you will find in the book.

Where are you?
On each map, a small **globe** shows where in the world the map is, and points north, south, east and west. This globe is called a locator.

Canada and the Arctic

Canada is the biggest country in the continent of North America and the second biggest in the world. Only Russia is larger. Canada's northern coast is on the Arctic Ocean that surrounds the North Pole. Every direction is south from the North Pole. The US state of Alaska borders the northwest of the country. Few Canadians live in the cold north. Most big cities, such as Toronto and Montreal, are in the warmer south, close to the border with the United States of America.

Did you know?

In the Inuit (say 'in-oo-it') language there are 20 different words that mean snow.

In 1848 the winter weather was so cold on the Canadian and United States border that it froze Niagara Falls.

There is no land at the North Pole. Frozen ocean surrounds it.

NORWAY

GREENLAND (DENMARK)

Arctic Circle

RUSSIA

North Pole

ARCTIC OCEAN

Ellesmere Island

Queen Elizabeth Islands

Banks Island

RUSSIA

Bering Strait

Alaska (USA)

ICELAND

NORTH ATLANTIC OCEAN

Newfoundland

Prince Edward Island

New Brunswick

Nova Scotia

Montreal
Ottawa

St Lawrence River

Quebec

Lake Ontario
Niagara Falls

Toronto

Lake Huron

Lake Erie

Lake Michigan

Lake Superior

Great Lakes

Baffin Island

Nunavut

(Inuit Territories)

CANADA

Hudson Bay

Ontario

Victoria Island

Nelson River

Lake Winnipeg

Manitoba

Great Bear Lake

Northwest Territories

Lake Athabasca

Churchill River

Great Slave Lake

Saskatchewan

Mackenzie River

Alberta

Calgary

Yukon Territory

Rocky Mountains

British Columbia

Vancouver

Vancouver Island

UNITED STATES OF AMERICA

S

S

S

S

Land on this map

mountains

grassland

deciduous forest

evergreen forest

tundra

ice and snow

Northern Canada and the Arctic

The Arctic is the northern-most **region** on Earth. The dark winter days are so cold that the land and the ocean stay frozen. From an aeroplane, the sea looks like a huge window of broken glass. Even in the middle of the short summer, the air **temperature** is often below freezing. Further south is the Canadian tundra. The Inuit (say "In-oo-it") people have lived in the Arctic and on the tundra for thousands of years.

▲ During an arctic winter the Inuit must dig through thick ice to find fresh water.

Animals and plants

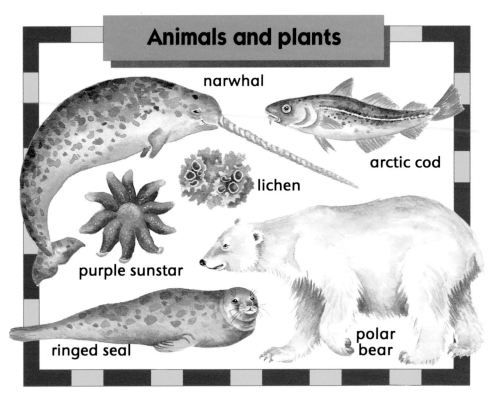

narwhal

arctic cod

lichen

purple sunstar

ringed seal

polar bear

The Inuit live in remote towns on the ice of the far north. They work in gold, tin and copper mines or fish for arctic cod. They travel by snowmobile or sled. The Inuit can find their way across the ice deserts without maps or **landmarks** to guide them.

Thousands of icebergs float in the Arctic and North Atlantic Oceans. They are enormous chunks of ice that break away from the edges of **glaciers**. Some are as big as mountains. Only the tip of the iceberg shows above the surface.

now picture this

An arctic iceberg once floated as far south as the island of Bermuda off the coast of North Carolina, USA.

▲ On long hunting trips the Inuit build igloos from slabs of ice. The igloo provides shelter during the long, cold nights.

◄ Skidoos or snowmobiles carry equipment and supplies across the arctic ice deserts.

Southern Canada

Wide open countryside of forests and lakes surrounds Canada's cities. In the Rocky Mountains in the west there are large national parks. The flat **plains** of Saskatchewan (say "Sas-catch-e-wan"), Alberta and Manitoba are east of the Rocky Mountains. These plains are Canada's prairies. Native Americans once hunted buffalo here. Now farmers keep cattle and grow fields of wheat.

The first Canadians were Inuit (say "In-oo-it") and Native Americans. Then other Europeans settled here. Most people in Quebec (say "Kwe-beck") in Southern Canada have French **ancestors**. Montreal is the largest French-speaking city in the world after Paris, France.

Vancouver is just one of southwestern Canada's many beautiful cities. Some, such as Medicine Hat, have names that are translated from Native American languages. Calgary, in southwestern Alberta, is the oil centre of Canada and the province's largest city.

▶ **Calgary is one of the fastest growing cities in Canada.**

Animals and plants

beaver

grizzly bear

maple

pine

moose

raccoon

Timber is one of Canada's biggest **industries**. The country has more evergreen forest than anywhere else in the world. Timber companies own enormous plantations of pine, spruce and larch trees. The wood is cut into logs or pulped to make paper.

▲ Some of the world's best ice hockey players are Canadian.

United States of America

The United States of America is a big country in North America. It is divided into 50 **states**. Its countryside is made up of hot deserts, thick forests, wide **plains**, lakes the size of seas, snow-capped mountains and deep **canyons**. There are also many modern cities. Native Americans have lived in the United States for thousands of years. Now, people from all over the world live and visit here, too.

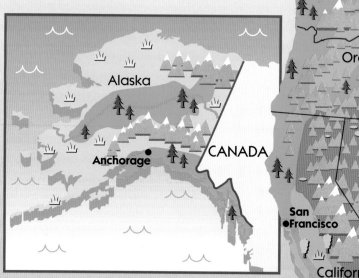

Did you know?

Winds can reach 370 kilometres per hour at the top of Mount Washington in New Hampshire.

Americans living near the bottom of the Grand Canyon have their post delivered by mule.

Mauna Kea, a **volcano** in Hawaii, is even taller than Mount Everest. But most of it lies under the sea.

Two states, Alaska and Hawaii, are not attached to the **mainland**. Alaska, the biggest state, is far north in the icy Arctic **region**. Hawaii is a long chain of **volcanic islands**. It is far west in the Pacific Ocean. We moved them on to this map so you could see all of the United States.

The Rio Grande, or Big River, separates Mexico from the United States. Mountain chains run along the west and east coasts of Mexico. The rest of the country is mainly dry desert. Most Mexicans live in the centre of Mexico and nearly seventeen million people live in the capital, Mexico City. It is the largest city in the world.

and Mexico

CANADA

Montana

North Dakota

Minnesota

Lake Superior

South Dakota

Wisconsin

Lake Huron

Mount Washington

Maine

Wyoming

Mount Rushmore

Michigan

Lake Michigan

Lake Ontario

Vermont

New Hampshire

Niagara Falls

STATES OF AMERICA

Chicago

Detroit

Lake Erie

New York

Boston

Connecticut

Massachusetts

Rhode Island

Rocky Mountains

Colorado River

Iowa

Nebraska

Indiana

Ohio

Pennsylvania

Philadelphia

New York

New Jersey

Delaware

Colorado

Kansas

Missouri River

Illinois

Missouri

Washington DC

West Virginia

Maryland

ATLANTIC OCEAN

Great Plains

Ohio River

Kentucky

Virginia

New Mexico

Oklahoma

Arkansas

Tennessee

Appalachian Mountains

North Carolina

N

Mississippi River

South Carolina

Dallas

Mississippi

Atlanta

Georgia

W

E

Texas

Louisiana

Alabama

Rio Grande

Houston

New Orleans

Florida

Kennedy Space Center

MEXICO

Gulf of Mexico

S

Miami

Land on this map

	desert		evergreen forest
	mountains		rainforest
	grassland		tundra
	deciduous forest		

Mexico City

Mount Popocatépetl

BELIZE

Acapulco

GUATEMALA

Northeast USA

The Northeast **region** of the United States includes the **states** of Maine, New Hampshire, Vermont, Rhode Island, Connecticut, Massachusetts (say 'mass-a-choo-sets'), New York, Pennsylvania and New Jersey. It is the most crowded part of the country. Here, it is warm in summer and cold in winter. Many people live in the big cities of New York, Philadelphia and Boston along the Atlantic coast.

The Northeast is the region in which Europeans first settled. Many people came here from England during the 1600s and 1700s.

▲ Winter in the Northeast can be very cold. These children live in Vermont, close to the Canadian border.

Small farms raise dairy cattle and grow apples on the **fertile plains** and hills of the Northeast. Fishermen catch cod, tuna and plaice along the Atlantic coast.

The city of New York is the largest in the United States. Many people here have jobs that serve the public, such as teaching, working in shops and restaurants, and driving taxi cabs and trains.

▲ The nation's oldest buildings are in the region of New England.

▼ The world's first skyscrapers were built on Manhattan Island in New York.

The Appalachian Trail runs from Maine to Georgia. It is the longest marked footpath in the world. You can walk along the Appalachian Mountains, through North Carolina and Virginia, to the snow-capped mountains of Maine and New Hampshire.

Animals and plants

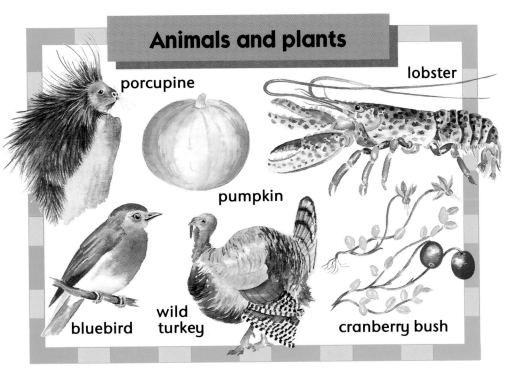

porcupine

lobster

pumpkin

bluebird

wild turkey

cranberry bush

▲ New York's Statue of Liberty stands for freedom.

Midwest and West USA

The Midwest forms a large **region** in the centre of the USA. It includes a vast, mostly flat area called the Great Plains and cities such as Chicago and Detroit around the five Great Lakes. The Rocky Mountains divide the Midwest from **states** such as Washington, Oregon, California and Nevada in the West. The west coast has rocky shores, vast forests and **fertile valleys**.

▼ The heads of American Presidents George Washington, Thomas Jefferson, Theodore Roosevelt and Abraham Lincoln are carved out of Mount Rushmore, in South Dakota.

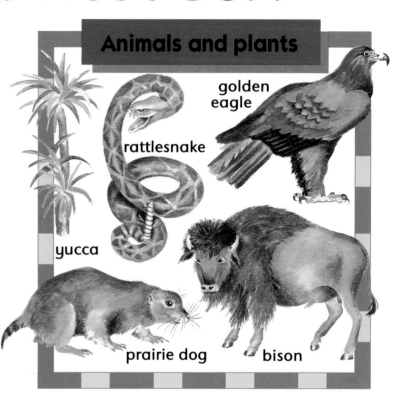

Animals and plants

golden eagle

rattlesnake

yucca

prairie dog

bison

The Midwest region is known as the 'farm belt'. Much of the land is flat **plains** called prairies. Many people here live on farms and grow wheat or raise cattle.

Barges, or narrow boats, carry soya beans, coal, iron and grain down the Mississippi River to the Gulf of Mexico. Here, the goods are loaded into large container ships and sent to other countries.

The continental divide is a long stretch of high ground that runs north and south through the Rocky Mountains. It separates the rivers that flow east from those that flow west.

Many people visit the Rocky Mountain states of Colorado and Wyoming for the good ski slopes and beautiful scenery.

▼ Monument Valley in Utah has red **sandstone** towers of rock that rise up to 40 metres.

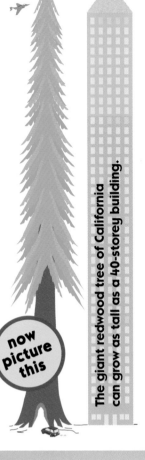

now picture this

The giant redwood tree of California can grow as tall as a 40-storey building.

▲ In New Mexico, silver is mined from the ground and made into beautiful jewellery.

California is the third largest state in the country. On its coast are big cities such as San Francisco and Los Angeles. Computers and wine-making are important **industries** here. In Hollywood, in Los Angeles, hundreds of films are made every year that are seen all over the world.

The South

▲ Kennedy Space Center is at Cape Canaveral in Florida. The first people to land on the Moon were launched in a rocket from here.

The warm and **fertile** South extends from Texas on the Gulf of Mexico, to Virginia on the Atlantic coast. This **region** produces much of the nation's fruit and vegetables. Cattle ranches and oil fields dot the southwestern **state** of Texas, the second largest of the United States.

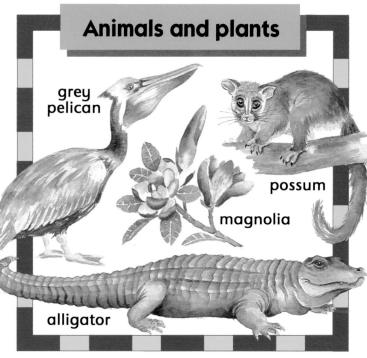

Animals and plants

grey pelican

possum

magnolia

alligator

Florida is the southern-most state in the country. Millions of people holiday here every year. They visit Disney World and go fishing. Many Americans move to Florida when they **retire**. Miami is Florida's biggest city. It did not exist one hundred years ago. It is now a centre of international business and banking.

Mexico

Mexico is a mountainous country south of the USA. More than half of all Mexicans are mestizos (say 'mes-tee-soes'). Their **ancestors** were Native Americans and Spanish. About 500 years ago, the Spanish came to Mexico in search of new lands. Here, they found Aztec people living in great cities. Modern Mexico City is built over the Aztec city of Tenochtitlan (say 'tay-nock-tee-tel-an'). Spanish is the official language of Mexico.

► Mexican craftworkers make and sell pottery, baskets and silver jewellery. They follow beautiful old Indian designs.

◄ These monuments form part of the remains of an ancient city called Chichen Itzá (say 'chi-chen-its-a').

Mexican farmers grow cotton, coffee, wheat and beans. Maize is their main food. It is used to make spicy pancakes, called tortillas (say 'tor-tee-yas').

The capital, Mexico City, is very crowded. If all the people who lived here joined hands they would form a human chain stretching half-way around the world.

Central and South America

Central America is a narrow bridge of mountainous land between North and South America. On its west is the Pacific Ocean, and on its east, the Atlantic Ocean. The Panama Canal provides a shortcut for ships sailing from one ocean to the other. To the east are the beautiful islands of the West Indies. Only the largest islands are named on this map.

Land on this map

- desert
- mountains
- rainforest
- evergreen forest
- grassland

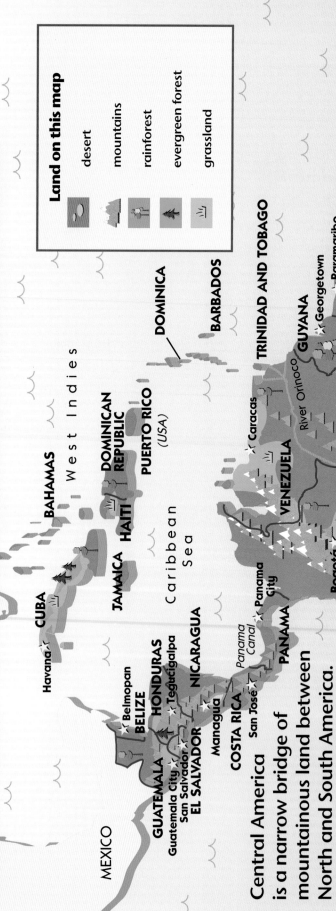

MEXICO

Havana
CUBA
BAHAMAS
West Indies

Belmopan
BELIZE
GUATEMALA
Guatemala City
San Salvador
EL SALVADOR
HONDURAS
Tegucigalpa
Managua
NICARAGUA
COSTA RICA
San José
Panama Canal
PANAMA
Panama City

JAMAICA
HAITI
DOMINICAN REPUBLIC
PUERTO RICO (USA)
Caribbean Sea
DOMINICA
BARBADOS
TRINIDAD AND TOBAGO

Caracas
VENEZUELA
River Orinoco
GUYANA
Georgetown
Paramaribo
SURINAM
Cayenne
FRENCH GUIANA

COLOMBIA
Bogotá
ECUADOR
Quito
PERU
Lima

River Amazon
Amazon Rainforest
BRAZIL

Equator

PACIFIC OCEAN

ATLANTIC OCEAN

Brasília ☆

River Sã

Rio de Janeiro
São Paulo

BOLIVIA

PARAGUAY

Asunción ☆

Gran Chaco

River Paraná

River Uruguay

URUGUAY

Montevideo ☆

La Paz ☆

Cusco
Lake
Titicaca

Atacama
Desert

Buenos
Aires ☆

Pampas

ARGENTINA

Santiago ☆

CHILE

Andes Mountains

Patagonia

Tierra del
Fuego
● Ushuaia

Cape Horn

FALKLAND
ISLANDS
(UK)

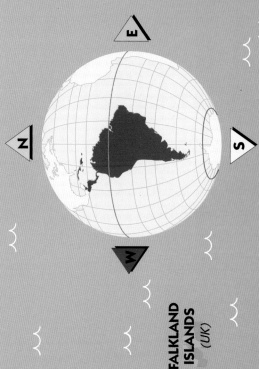

N
E
S
W

Did you know?

Every 60 seconds, farmers of the rainforest burn areas of forest as big as 160 football pitches.

Howler monkeys of Central America are the noisiest animals in the world. Their jungle calls can be heard 16 kilometres away.

The ancient Inca peoples had so much gold that the richest of them had combs and knives made from it.

The continent of South America is shaped like a long triangle. Most of it is south of the Equator. The southern tip lies close to the icy continent of Antarctica. Along the west coast are the high, cold Andes Mountains. South America's biggest country is Brazil. Here, the River Amazon flows through the largest tropical rainforest in the world.

Central America

The seven countries of Panama, Guatemala, Belize, Honduras, Costa Rica, El Salvador and Nicaragua form **mainland** Central America. Here, there are active **volcanoes**, heavy rains and **earthquakes**. The south of the **region** has thick tropical rainforest and few roads. The easiest way through to the continent of South America is by aeroplane.

Animals and plants

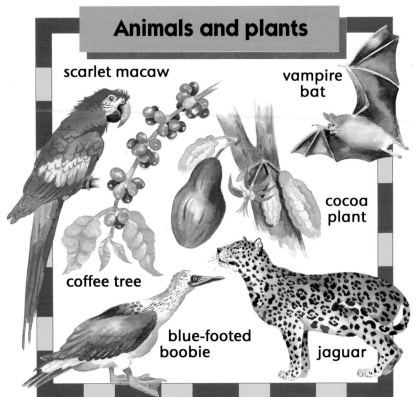

scarlet macaw

vampire bat

cocoa plant

coffee tree

blue-footed boobie

jaguar

▲ These women weave wool for sale at a Guatemalan market. They are **descended** from an ancient people called the Maya.

Almost all Central Americans speak Spanish. Many are poor farmers living on small farms. Others work on cotton, coffee or banana plantations.

Some farmers cut down and burn large areas of the forest. They grow maize on this land. After a few years they move on. Then cattle ranchers graze their herds on the cleared-out land. The forest has no time to grow back, so wild animals lose their homes.

The West Indies

Some West Indian islands, such as the Bahamas, Barbados and Jamaica, are perfect for a holiday, and many West Indian people work in the tourist **industry**. Others fish, grow tropical fruits or work on large coffee, banana and sugar plantations.

▼ Workers cut the fruit from banana palms in Dominica.

▼ This beautiful beach, made of white, **coral** sand, is on the West Indian island of Tobago.

Tropical South America

Brazil, Venezuela, Surinam, French Guiana (say "Ghee-an-a") and Guyana make up most of tropical South America. They are hot, wet countries covered with rainforest, except for eastern Brazil, where there are areas of rich grassland. The mighty River Amazon flows through the rainforest to the Atlantic Ocean. Further south, along the coast, are many big, modern cities.

Most people in this **region** live in the east coast cities and towns. But a few groups of native peoples still live deep in the Amazon rainforest. They have their own languages and customs and use feathers, flowers and seeds to decorate their bodies. Even their building materials and medicines come from the forest.

▶ Plant dyes are used to make the body paint decorating this Kanelo Indian boy.

▼ Yanomami hunters tip their arrows with deadly animal poisons.

▲ Rio de Janeiro, in Brazil, is the second largest city in South America after São Paulo.

Carnival time

For several days every autumn a huge party is held in cities in tropical South America. People dress in colourful costumes and dance to samba music.

▶ Carnival takes place before Easter each year and lasts for four days and nights.

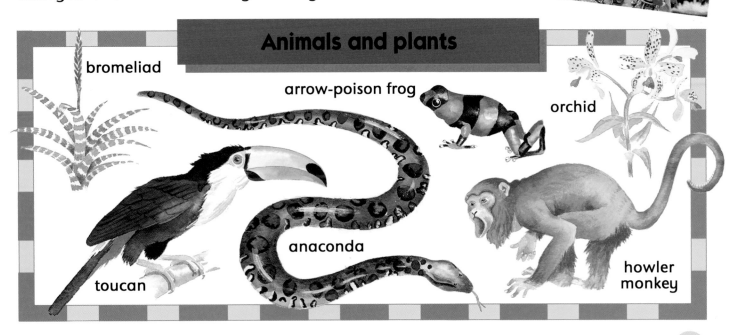

Animals and plants

bromeliad

arrow-poison frog

orchid

toucan

anaconda

howler monkey

The Countries of the Andes

The countries of Colombia, Ecuador, Peru, Bolivia and Chile are in the Andes **region** of South America (say 'eck-wa-door' and 'chill-ee'). The Andes Mountains are over 7,200 kilometres long. They run along the length of western South America. Many of the mountains are active **volcanoes**. About half the people who live in this region are Native American Indians called Quechas (say 'ketch-as').

▶ The ruins of Machu Picchu are on a mountain top, near Cusco in the Andes. This great walled city was built by the ancient Inca people about 500 years ago.

La Paz, the capital of Bolivia, is more than three kilometres above sea level. It is the highest large city in the world. Here it is too cold for crops or trees to grow. The world's highest **navigable** lake is nearby. It is called Lake Titicaca.

◀ People who live around Lake Titicaca build their houses entirely from reeds that grow beside the lake.

In Peru, Bolivia and Ecuador, mountain farmers grow beans, **gourds**, potatoes and maize. They keep llamas and alpacas for their wool and meat. Gold, silver and copper are mined.

The Atacama Desert, in Chile, lies between the Pacific coast and the Andes Mountains. It is the driest desert in the world, with almost no plants or people. In 1971 a part of this northern desert had its first rainfall in 400 years!

▼ Fresh fruit and vegetables are brought by lorry to this Bolivian market from the warm, **fertile valleys** below the mountains.

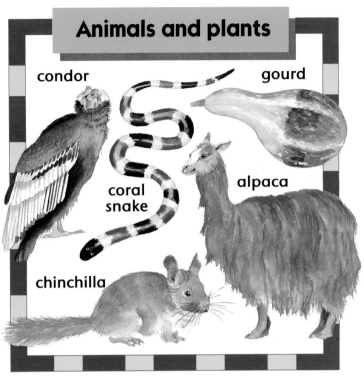

Animals and plants

condor

gourd

coral snake

alpaca

chinchilla

Southern South America

Paraguay, Uruguay, Argentina and southern Chile make up Southern South America, (say 'par-a-gwy', 'yur-uh-gwy' and 'chill-ee'). Rich grasslands, called pampas, cover large areas of land. Thousands of sheep and cattle graze on huge cattle stations here. The north of the **region** is warm and dry, but the southern tip is cold and stormy. It is called Tierra del Fuego (say 'tee-err-a del fway-go'). This means 'land of fire' in Spanish.

▼ In Argentina, cowboys called gauchos (say 'gow-chose') round up cattle on the pampas.

A dry, windy **plain** called the Gran Chaco covers much of Paraguay. Few people live here. Most live in cities or work on farms, growing soya beans, peanuts or cotton. Most of Uruguay is pampas.

Argentina is the biggest country in the southern part of the continent. Many Argentinians are **descended** from European settlers. One third live in its capital, Buenos Aires. On the pampas of central Argentina, farmers grow wheat and maize, and cattle ranches cover hundreds of kilometres.

▼ Cold winds from Antarctica bring snow and ice to Patagonia.

now picture this

If you sailed east around the world from Ushuaia you would end up back where you started without ever seeing land.

The Patagonia region of Argentina is high and windy. There are no trees. Just a few sheep farmers live here. In the far south there are snow-capped **volcanoes**, **geysers**, lakes, waterfalls and islands. The town of Ushuaia (say 'oo-shoo-ay-ah'), near stormy Cape Horn, is further south than any other town in the world.

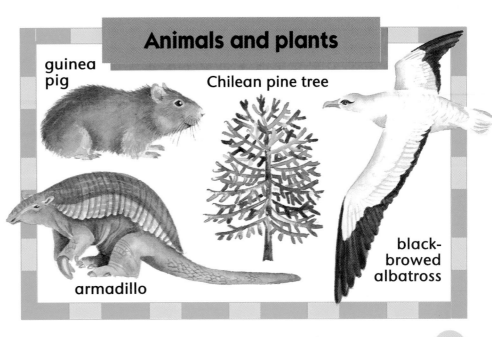

Animals and plants

guinea pig

Chilean pine tree

black-browed albatross

armadillo

Africa

The huge continent of Africa has over 50 countries. More than 1,000 languages are spoken here. Africa is hot almost everywhere. The hottest place in the world is the vast Sahara Desert in the north. Further south, thick rainforest lies close to the Equator. Rich grasslands cover much of East and Southern Africa.

Did you know?

The horns of the African rhinoceros are made not of ivory but of very tough, compressed hair.

The hottest place in the world is Al-Aziziyah in Libya. One day in 1922 it was over 58° **Celsius** in the shade!

In East Africa, the Masai (say 'mass-eye') people drink a mixture of cow's blood and milk.

Canary Islands (SPAIN)

WESTERN SAHARA
Laayoune
MOROCCO
Rabat
Fez
Atlas Mountains
Algiers
Tunis
TUNISIA
Tripoli
Al-Aziziyah
LIBYA
Mediterranean Sea
Giza
Cairo
EGYPT
River Nile
Red Sea
ERITREA

MAURITANIA
Nouakchott
MALI
River Niger
ALGERIA
Sahara Desert
NIGER
CHAD

38

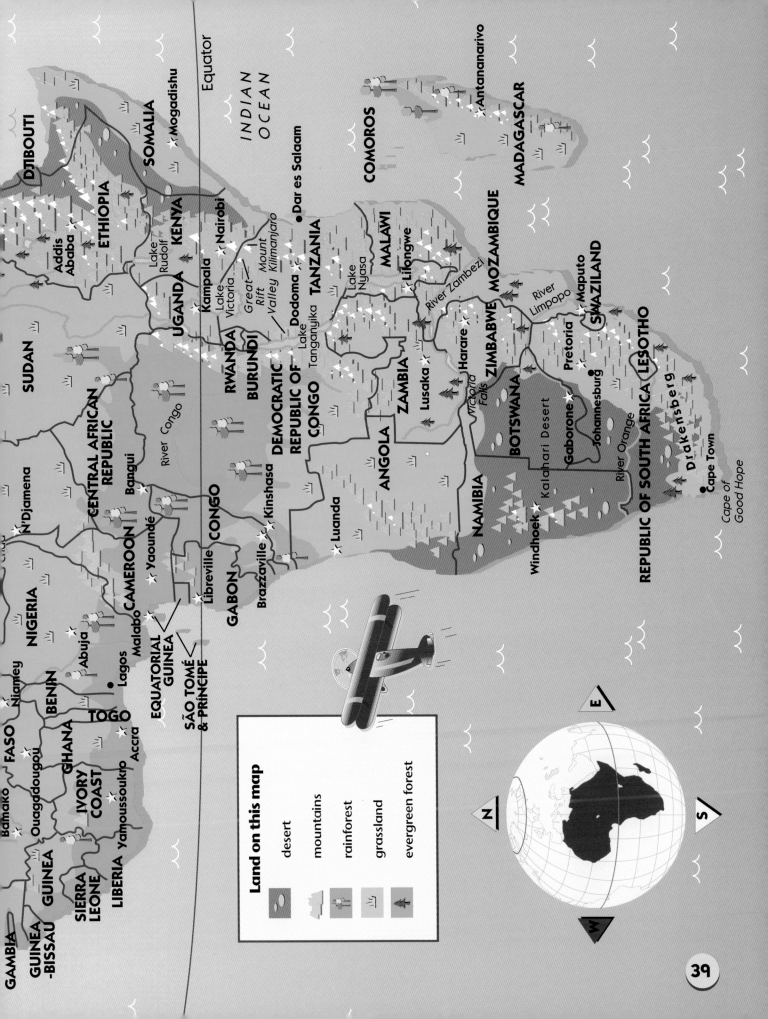

GAMBIA

GUINEA -BISSAU

GUINEA

SIERRA LEONE

LIBERIA

Bamako

Niamey

Ouagadougou

FASO

BENIN

IVORY COAST

GHANA

TOGO

Yamoussoukro

Accra

Lagos

Abuja

NIGERIA

N'Djamena

Lomé

DJIBOUTI

SOMALIA

Mogadishu

ETHIOPIA

Addis Ababa

SUDAN

CENTRAL AFRICAN REPUBLIC

Bangui

CAMEROON

Yaoundé

Malabo

EQUATORIAL GUINEA

SÃO TOMÉ & PRINCIPE

Libreville

GABON

CONGO

Brazzaville

Kinshasa

Luanda

DEMOCRATIC REPUBLIC OF CONGO

River Congo

RWANDA

BURUNDI

UGANDA

KENYA

Kampala

Nairobi

Lake Rudolf

Lake Victoria

Mount Kilimanjaro

Great Rift Valley

Dodoma

Dar es Salaam

TANZANIA

Lake Tanganyika

ANGOLA

ZAMBIA

Lusaka

Lake Nyasa

MALAWI

Lilongwe

River Zambezi

Victoria Falls

Harare

ZIMBABWE

Pretoria

Johannesburg

River Limpopo

Maputo

SWAZILAND

MOZAMBIQUE

COMOROS

Antananarivo

MADAGASCAR

NAMIBIA

BOTSWANA

Windhoek

Gaborone

Kalahari Desert

River Orange

REPUBLIC OF SOUTH AFRICA

LESOTHO

Drakensberg

Cape Town

Cape of Good Hope

Equator

INDIAN OCEAN

Land on this map

desert

mountains

rainforest

grassland

evergreen forest

N

E

S

W

North Africa

The Sahara Desert covers a large part of North Africa. In most years, there is almost no rain here. This means that water for people, plants and animals is hard to find. Much of the desert is flat, stony **plain**, but in the middle are great **sand dunes** as high as mountains. Most North Africans live in villages and towns along the Mediterranean coast, where they can catch fish and there is enough rain in winter to grow fruit and vegetables.

▲ The people of Niger build desert wells to provide water for their crops and animals.

Many North Africans live in towns of flat-roofed houses that have thick walls to keep out the heat. The Bedouin (say "Bed-oo-win") desert **nomads** are people who live in the hot, dry desert. They move from place to place to find water for themselves and their animals.

Animals and plants

jerboa

camel

scorpion

cactus

fennec fox

now picture this

The Great Pyramid at Giza in Egypt was built from two million blocks of stone. Some were as heavy as three African elephants!

The Bedouin wear long, loose clothes to protect them from the sun. Their camels and goats can go without water for longer than cows and sheep. Bedouin take their water from **oases**. These are pools of water that bubble up from under the ground to the desert surface. People and animals can take shelter in the shade of date palms that grow around the oases.

▶ This leather worker in the city of Fez, Morocco, soaks animal hides in vats filled with tanning solutions. These are special dyes that keep the leather waterproof.

▼ The Nile is the longest river in the world. In Egypt it provides water to **irrigate** the farmland on its banks.

West Africa

Several countries, including Senegal, Ghana and Nigeria, make up West Africa. Some, such as Togo and Gambia, are very small. Their **fertile** land is used to farm coffee, cocoa, rubber, fruit and palm oil. Important **industries** are mining and **textiles**, oil and timber production.

Nigeria, in West Africa, has more people than any other country in Africa. Lagos (say 'lay-goss'), the largest city, is its industrial centre. Oil provides Nigerians with money to start modern, new industries such as clothing, food products, steel production and car **manufacturing**.

▲ These bowls are made from **gourds** that grow on climbing vines.

Central Africa

Many countries, from Cameroon to the Democratic Republic of Congo form Central Africa. On each side of the River Congo is an enormous area of thick, tropical rainforest. There are very few roads. People travel by riverboat or in canoes hollowed out from hardwood trees. They live in villages and towns in small clearings in the fast-growing forest.

Some riverboats on the River Congo are so crowded they are like a moving town. They carry a market, chemist, barber and police. The boat serves people for hundreds of kilometres along the river.

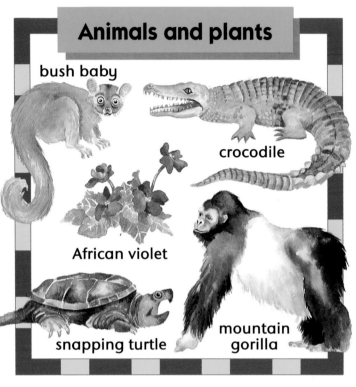

Animals and plants

bush baby

crocodile

African violet

snapping turtle

mountain gorilla

▼ This city in Democratic Republic of Congo is built of mud.

East Africa

▼ There may be up to 30 lions living in one group, or pride, on the East African grassland.

East Africa is made up of eight countries, from Ethiopia, Somalia and Eritrea (say "Air-i-tray-a") in the north, to Tanzania in the south. The mountains and high, flat grasslands of some of these countries make them cooler than others near the Equator. Long grass and scattered trees cover much of East Africa. This type of land is called savannah. In the north, Somalia and parts of Ethiopia are very dry. Here there is often drought, which is when there is no rain to grow crops.

East Africans are made up of many different groups such as the Turkana, Masai and Kikuyu (say "Mass-eye" and "Kick-oo-you"). They are farmers, fishermen, craftworkers or workers in city **industries**. Village people often live in large family groups that include uncles, aunts, cousins and grandparents.

The Great Rift Valley divides the land of East Africa. The **valley** was formed by **earthquakes** millions of years ago. In some places it is 600 metres deep.

Near the Great Rift Valley are East Africa's large game reserves. These are areas where protected wild animals such as the lion, leopard, rhinoceros, giraffe, elephant and many others can roam freely. But although it is against the law, **poachers** sometimes kill the animals for their skins, horns or tusks.

▶ The Masai (say "Mass-eye") hold the world record for the highest standing jump.

Animals and plants

cheetah

acacia

pangolin

guinea fowl

flamingo

zebra

Southern Africa

Southern Africa extends south from Angola, Zambia and Malawi and includes the island country of Madagascar. In the east are high, flat grasslands and deep **valleys**. Two of the great African rivers, the Zambezi (say "Zam-bee-zee") and the Limpopo are here. The hot, dry Kalahari Desert is in the west, along the Atlantic Coast. Most Southern African countries are hot and sunny all year round.

The countries of Angola, Zambia and Zimbabwe (say "Zim-bahb-wee") are rich in minerals, including diamonds, gold, iron and copper. The wealthy country of South Africa has the richest diamond and gold mines in the world.

▲ Mine workers in Zambia drill for copper hundreds of metres below ground.

Animals and plants

aardvark

ostrich

baobab

welwitschsia

white rhino

lemur

South Africa's modern cities and large factories attract people from poorer African countries. They come to find work in the cities of Cape Town and Johannesburg. For years, people had to obey a law called apartheid (say "a-par-tide"). This meant black people had to live in separate towns and go to different schools from white people. Now apartheid has ended. Blacks and whites will run their country together.

▼ Cape Town lies at the tip of South Africa.

In the Kalahari Desert there is little water for crops and animals. The San people, who live here, hunt wild animals and gather honey and fruit for food.

now picture this

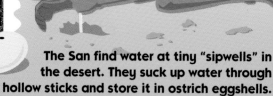

The San find water at tiny "sipwells" in the desert. They suck up water through hollow sticks and store it in ostrich eggshells.

▼ In the island country of Madagascar, women and children grind grain to make flour.

Europe

The continent of Europe is bordered by the Arctic and Atlantic oceans in the north and west, and the Mediterranean Sea in the south. It is the only continent in the world without a desert. Mountains, forests, rivers and fields surround its cities, towns and villages. There are more than 40 countries in Europe. Each has its own languages, foods and history.

Arctic Circle

Lapland

FINLAND

Helsinki

Tallinn

ESTONIA

LATVIA

Riga

LITHUANIA

Vilnius

Kaliningrad
(Russia)

SWEDEN

Gulf of Bothnia

Stockholm

Baltic Sea

POLAND

Warsaw

Prague

NORWAY

Oslo

DENMARK

Copenhagen

Berlin

GERMANY

LUXEMBOURG

North Sea

NETHERLANDS

Amsterdam

BELGIUM

Brussels

Paris

River

ICELAND

Reykjavik

REPUBLIC OF IRELAND

Dublin

Northern Ireland
(UK)

UNITED KINGDOM

London

English Channel

ATLANTIC OCEAN

Did you know?

Over five million years ago, the Mediterranean Sea was dry land. Now this large sea is only connected to the Atlantic Ocean by a narrow strait. But the sea is slowly closing up. In a few million years, it may disappear completely.

Only about 1,000 people live in the smallest country in the world. It is Vatican City, part of Rome, in Italy.

Northern Europe

▼ Norway's coastline has many long, narrow inlets of sea water. They are called fjords (say "fee-yords").

The countries of Norway, Sweden, Finland, Lithuania, Estonia, Latvia, Denmark and Iceland make up Northern Europe. Here it is very cold in winter and cool in summer. The land in the far north is bare and rocky. South of the Arctic Circle are jagged mountains, forests and lakes. In the far south are the cities, towns and villages where most people live.

The Arctic Circle, that circles the top of the world, crosses Northern Europe about 2,600 kilometres south of the North Pole. It divides the cold, north polar **region** from the warmer lands south of it. Land near the Arctic Circle is too rugged for farming. People catch fish to eat instead. Few animals can find enough food to survive the cold winters here.

Animals and plants

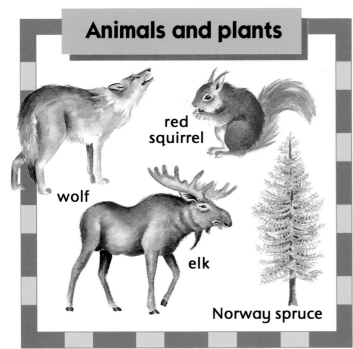

wolf

red squirrel

elk

Norway spruce

Northern Europe is an important producer of wood. Spruce, larch and pine trees are cut down and used to build homes and to make furniture, toys, matches and paper.

▼ Legoland is a Danish theme park where visitors can walk around models of world-famous buildings made from plastic bricks.

Part of northern Finland and Sweden is named Lapland. The **nomadic** Sami live here and keep reindeer for their milk, meat and leather.

▶ The Sami often wear brightly coloured costumes decorated with beads. Their sleighs take tourists for rides across the frozen tundra.

51

Western Europe

The countries of Western Europe lie between Northern Europe in the north and the Mediterranean Sea in the south. Most of the **region** is warmed by a current of ocean water called the Gulf Stream. This keeps the weather mild and wet. The countryside is divided into fields where crops are grown and cattle graze. The Alps are in the south of the region. Some of these mountains are over 4,000 metres high. Western Europe is one of the most important **industrial** areas in the world.

▼ The Alps cover most of Switzerland. Here, many children can ski by the age of seven.

▼ In London, the Queen inspects her troops at the ceremony of 'Trooping the Colour'.

In Western Europe's busy towns and cities, factory workers produce cars, dishwashers, glass, chocolate and many other goods. But some of the factories and machines cause pollution, which makes the air, rivers and even the ocean dirty. Pollution is a problem for people in cities around the world. They have to find ways of stopping it.

Busy streets

Tourists from all over the world visit European cities to see their ancient buildings and learn about European traditions. Although city centres can be crowded, the countryside is quieter. Wild animals and plants live undisturbed in fields and forests here.

▶ Shoppers and tourists fill the narrow streets of Amsterdam in the Netherlands.

Animals and plants

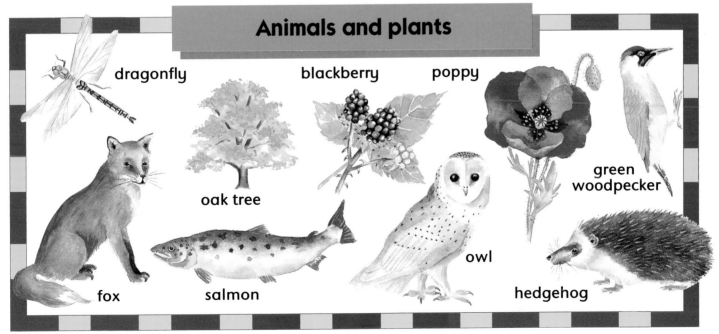

dragonfly

blackberry

poppy

oak tree

green woodpecker

owl

fox

salmon

hedgehog

The Mediterranean

▼ This village is on the **volcanic island** of Santorini, in Greece.

The European countries of Spain, France, Italy and Greece border the Mediterranean Sea. People have lived around its shores for thousands of years. The ruins of buildings from the **civilizations** of ancient Greece and Rome are found here. Some of these monuments and temples are more than 2,000 years old.

Hot, sunny Mediterranean summers attract millions of tourists. People holiday in towns, villages and resorts along the coast. Farming and fishing are also major **industries**. Markets in Mediterranean towns are full of fresh fruits and vegetables such as peppers, tomatoes and aubergines, and fish such as sardines and squid.

Mediterranean farmers grow olive trees. They gather the olives in the autumn and press them to make olive oil. The hot sun also makes it easy to grow grapes for wine, and juicy fruits such as oranges and melons.

▼ This outdoor market in southern Italy attracts shoppers with its colourful displays of fresh vegetables.

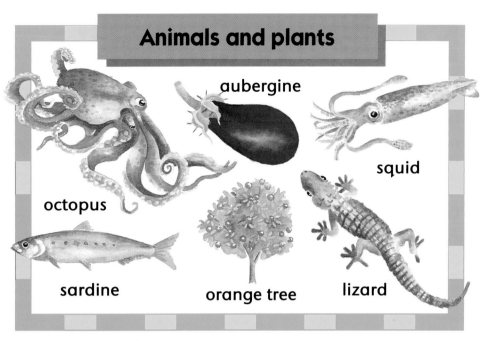

Animals and plants

octopus

aubergine

squid

sardine

orange tree

lizard

55

Russia and its neighbours

Russia is the largest country in the world. It is so big that it stretches across two continents, Europe and Asia. When it is breakfast time in western Russia, it is late afternoon in the east. Vast forests, mountains, farmland, plains and desert cover the lands of Russia and its neighbours. Most Russians live and work on farms and in factories in the west. Many people who live in neighbouring smaller countries are farmers.

St Petersburg

Minsk

BELARUS

MOLDOVA

Chisnau ☆ Kiev

Moscow

UKRAINE

European Russia

Black Sea

River Volga

s t e p p e

Ural Mountains

R

GEORGIA

Yerevan ☆ T'bilisi

ARMENIA

River Irtysh

AZERBAIJAN

☆ Baku

Caspian Sea

Aral Sea

KAZAKHSTAN

Astana ☆

TURKMENISTAN

Kara Kum Desert

Lake Balkash

Ashgabat

UZBEKISTAN

Tashkent ☆

Bishkek

Dushanbe

KYRGYZSTAN

TAJIKISTAN

N

W

E

S

Land on this map

 evergreen forest

 grassland

 mountains

 desert

 tundra

 deciduous forest

ARCTIC
OCEAN

Arctic Circle

Did you know?

Oymyakon is the world's coldest town. The **temperature** often drops to -46° Celcius.

Lake Baikal is the deepest lake in the world. If 950 people stood on each other's shoulders in the lake, the water would still cover them.

It takes seven days to travel on the Trans-Siberian Railway from Moscow in western Russia to Vladivostock in the east.

S i b e r i a

S I A

Oymyakon •

Asian Russia

River Yenisei

River Lena

Sea of
Okhotsk

t a i g a

Lake
Baikal

Trans-Siberian Railway

Vladivostock •

West of the Urals

The Ural Mountains divide Russia into two areas. The smaller, European part is in the west. Shipbuilding, steel production and coal mining are important **industries** here, but there are also large areas of **fertile** farmland. South and west of European Russia are some of its neighbours. They include the **independent countries** of Ukraine, Georgia and Azerbaijan (say 'az-er-by-jan'). In these countries many people live and work on farms.

Although Russia has many industries, the machinery in its factories is old and operates poorly. The Russians have to build new factories to make washing machines, clothes and other things people want to buy.

▲ In Moscow, the capital of Russia, people watch dancers in colourful traditional dress perform Russian folk dances.

Animals and plants

marbled polecat

lemming

mink

sturgeon

larch tree

World-famous dancers
Some of the greatest ballet music and dancers have come from Russia. The Kirov, Moscow City and Bolshoi Ballets perform all over the world.

Like the countries of Eastern Europe, Russia and its neighbours used to be ruled by a form of government called **Communism**. Russia's farms were so huge at that time that food did not get to the shops quickly enough and much of it rotted along the way.

Now people are choosing new kinds of government and the farms are being broken up into smaller ones. But in the cities, people still have to queue for hours just to buy a loaf of bread.

◀ Like many Russian churches, St Basil's Cathedral in Moscow has brightly painted, onion-shaped domes.

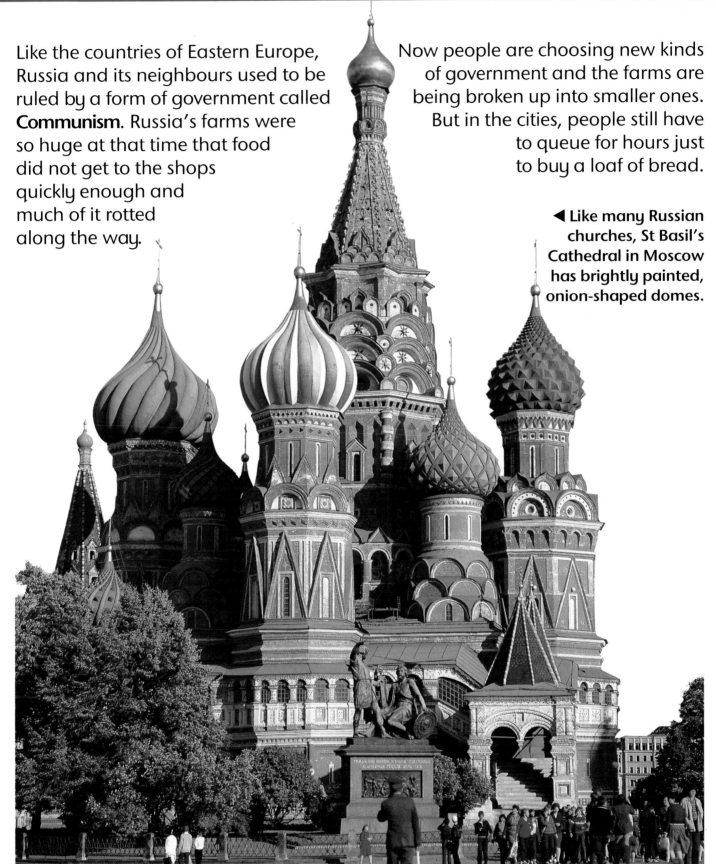

East of the Urals

East of the Ural Mountains is a huge area of Russia called Siberia. Most of Siberia is wilderness. It is too cold and stony for anything to grow except grass or trees. In the south is a huge forest of pine and fir named taiga (say 'tie-ga'). It is the largest forest in the world and bears and wolves roam wild here. Many people east of the Urals live on farms in countries next to the Caspian Sea and around the Aral Sea.

Rich mineral resources lie underground in Siberia. Here workers mine diamonds, gold, silver and copper. In neighbouring Uzbekistan (say 'uz-bek-i-stan'), they drill for oil and mine coal.

Animals and plants

snowy owl

Siberian tiger

hamster

silver birch tree

marmot

lynx

walrus

▼ The long, cold winters and frozen ground make work very difficult in Siberian mining towns.

▼ **Nomadic** herders in Central Siberia follow their reindeer from place to place as the animals search for food.

In the **independent countries** southwest of Siberian Russia, cotton, rice and silk are produced. In Turkmenistan's Kara Kum Desert people grow fruit around green and **fertile oases**.

The steppe is a vast **plain** of grassland and farmland west of Siberia. There are no trees. On the steppe wild hamsters and marmots take shelter from hot sun and icy winds in their underground burrows.

▶ The nearest city is hundreds of kilometres away from this Siberian farmer. She raises chickens for her eggs and meat.

Southwest and Southern

Did you know?

Mount Everest, in the Himalayas, is the highest mountain in the world above sea level. It is nearly 9 kilometres high.

In parts of northern India, Sikh men wear a kind of hat called a turban. It is made from a piece of material 12 metres long, which is wound around the head.

TURKEY
Ankara ★

Caspian Sea

Nicosia ★
CYPRUS
LEBANON
Beirut ★
ISRAEL
Jerusalem ★ ★ Amman
Dead Sea
JORDAN

SYRIA
★ Damascus

River Tigris

River Euphrates

Tehran ★

★ Baghdad

IRAQ

KUWAIT

Persian Gu

SAUDI
ARABIA

BAHRAIN

QAT

Riyadh ★

Mecca ●

Red Sea

Empty Quarter

YEMEN

San'a ★

AFRICA

Southwest and Southern Asia are parts of the huge continent of Asia. They are bordered by the Mediterranean and Red Seas in the west and are cut off from China by the Himalayas in the east. Southwest Asia is also called the Middle East. India is the biggest country in Southern Asia. Its cities are crowded and colourful, but most Indians live in villages in the countryside.

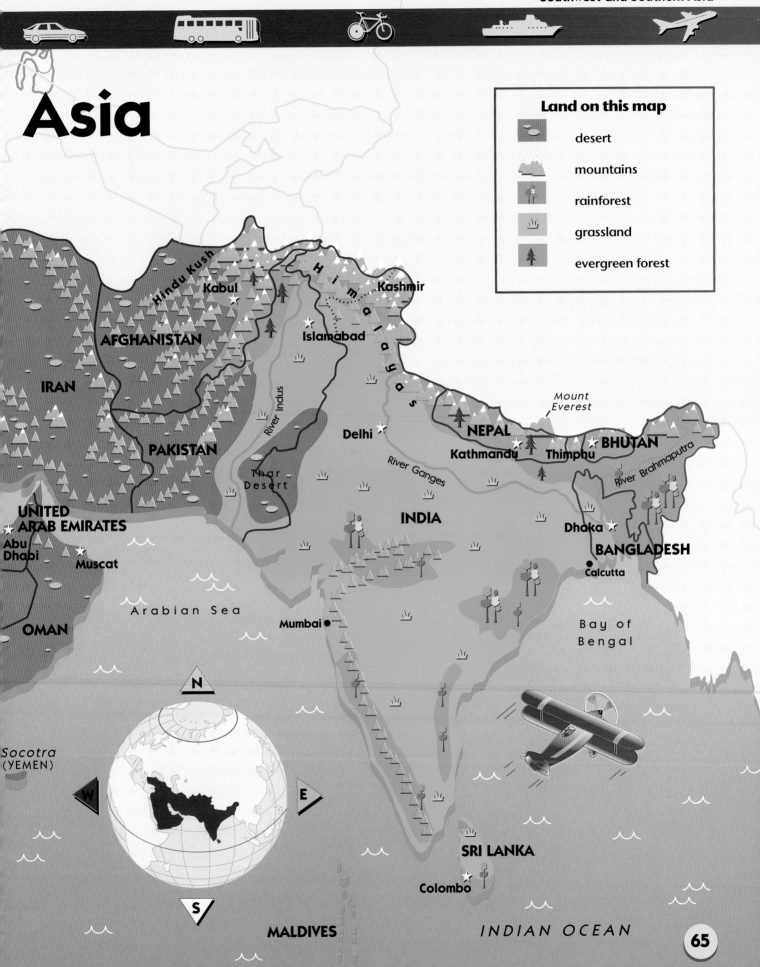

Asia

Land on this map

- desert
- mountains
- rainforest
- grassland
- evergreen forest

Hindu Kush

Kabul

Kashmir

AFGHANISTAN

H i m a l a y a s

Islamabad

IRAN

Mount Everest

River Indus

Delhi

NEPAL

PAKISTAN

Kathmandu

Thimphu

BHUTAN

Thar Desert

River Ganges

River Brahmaputra

UNITED ARAB EMIRATES

INDIA

Dhaka

Abu Dhabi

BANGLADESH

Muscat

Calcutta

Arabian Sea

Mumbai

Bay of Bengal

OMAN

N

Socotra (YEMEN)

W

E

SRI LANKA

S

Colombo

MALDIVES

INDIAN OCEAN

Southwest Asia

Large areas of Southwest Asia are hot, empty desert. Oil from wells and natural gas drilled from beneath the ground are the most important products of the desert countries. Crops can grow only around desert **oases** and water holes. But the land between the Tigris and Euphrates (say 'u-frate-ees') rivers is rich and **fertile**. This is where, thousands of years ago, people first began to settle and farm.

▲ Kuwait was once a poor desert country. But oil was discovered here and now it has many expensive new buildings.

Animals and plants

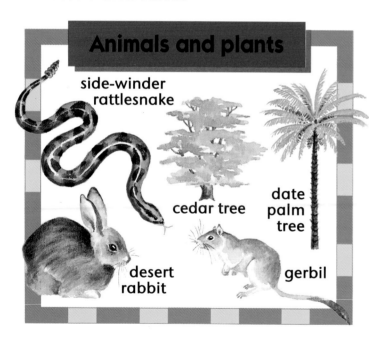

side-winder rattlesnake

cedar tree

date palm tree

desert rabbit

gerbil

Countries around the Persian Gulf sell oil to people around the world. This has made people here very rich. The oil is made into petrol, nylon and even soap. Millions of litres of petrol are burnt in the world's cars every day.

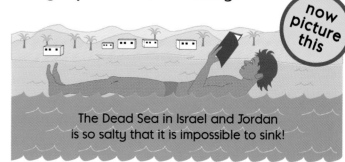

now picture this

The Dead Sea in Israel and Jordan is so salty that it is impossible to sink!

Three of the world's great **religions** began in Southwest Asia. The religion of the Jews is called Judaism and was started by Abraham 4,000 years ago. Christianity began 2,000 years ago. Muhammad founded the religion of Islam in Arabia about 600 years later. Today, these religions have followers all over the world.

▶ The Kuchi are **nomads** who live in the high, bare mountains of Afghanistan.

▼ Muslims follow the religion of Islam. They pray facing Mecca, their most holy city, which is in western Saudi Arabia.

Southern Asia

About three-quarters of the people in Southern Asia live in villages. Many farmers still use hand ploughs pulled by oxen or water buffalo. India has the biggest railway system in the world and more banks than any other country. Big cities, such as Mumbai and Delhi, are crowded with people, cars, bikes and animals.

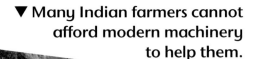

▼ Many Indian farmers cannot afford modern machinery to help them.

It is nearly always hot and dry in Southern Asia. But every summer the monsoon comes. This is a hot wind from the Indian Ocean that brings heavy rain. Rivers overflow and **flood** village streets and farms. But people welcome the monsoon because the rain helps their rice crops grow.

◄ The world-famous Taj Mahal in the north of India is built entirely from a hard, white rock called marble.

▶ Thousands of Indians come to bathe in the River Ganges in India. They believe the river waters are holy.

Most Indian farmers live in villages of mud and straw huts. Each home has only one or two rooms. The family sleeps on cots of woven string. Women often have to fetch water from wells in clay pots. They carry the full pots balanced on their heads.

The largest Indian cities are important centres of business and trade. The country's film **industry** is the biggest in the world.

Animals and plants

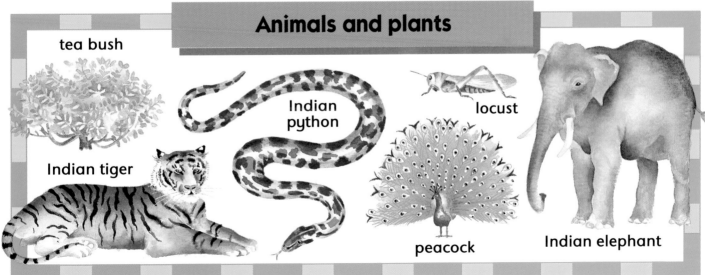

tea bush

Indian python

locust

Indian tiger

peacock

Indian elephant

China, Japan

China has one of the oldest **civilizations** in the world. It is part of Asia, but high mountains cut it off from the rest of the continent. About one fifth of the world's people live along China's east coast and in the **valleys** where the **climate** is warm and wet. Yet most of this country is empty desert and mountains.

Ulan Bat

MONGOLIA

Gobi Dese

Takla Makan Desert

Great Wall of China

Did you know?

In Mongolia and parts of western China, people put salt in their tea.

The Great Wall of China is the only thing built by people that can be seen from the Moon.

The air over the Takla Makan Desert is so hot that raindrops dry up before they hit the ground.

H i m a l a y a s

T i b e t

Mount Everest

N

W

E

S

Land on this map

 grassland   mountains

 rainforest   desert

 evergreen forest   tundra

70

and North and South Korea

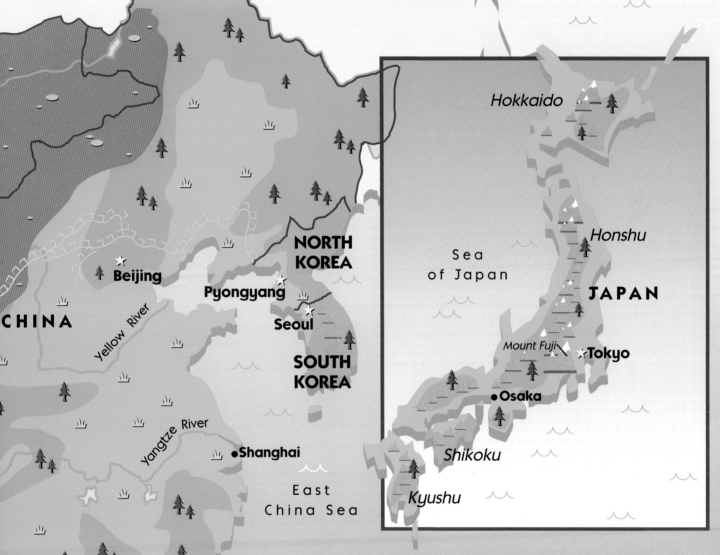

Hokkaido

Honshu

Sea
of Japan

JAPAN

Mount Fuji ★**Tokyo**

**NORTH
KOREA**

Pyongyang ★

★**Seoul**

**SOUTH
KOREA**

★ **Beijing**

CHINA

Yellow River

Yangtze River

●**Shanghai**

East
China Sea

●**Osaka**

Shikoku

Kyushu

Taipei ★

TAIWAN

Macao ● ●**Hong
Kong**

South
China Sea

**Hainan
(China)**

Japanese people call their country Nippon.
This means 'source of the sun'. It is a small
country, made up of four big islands and
4,000 small ones. It is shown larger on this
map than it should be. **Earthquakes** often
shake this mountainous land. North and South
Korea are in eastern Asia. Most Koreans live
on the coastal **plains** or in river valleys where
the climate is mild and the land is **fertile**.

China and Taiwan

China is the most populated country in the world. Over one thousand million people live here. China's government tries to make sure everyone has a job and a place to live. It also controls the wages that people earn and many of the prices that they pay for goods. Today, most Chinese people can afford to buy television sets, motorbikes and even build their own homes. But some village houses still have no running water or electricity.

Animals and plants

golden pheasant

yak

giant panda

bamboo

Bactrian camel

▲ This woman is selling noodles. These are thin strips of dough which are boiled in water.

The weather is warm and wet in crowded east China. Millions of people work on the land. They grow rice, which is the main food for most of them. Fields called paddies are **flooded** with water to help the rice crop grow. Water buffalo pull the ploughs. Some people live in small, thatch-roofed farmhouses made of mud bricks. Glass is still expensive, so many homes have paper windows.

Hong Kong is made up of a strip of **mainland** and over 200 islands. It is a major port on the southern coast of China. Its city is jammed with skyscrapers and blocks of flats.

Hong Kong factories make cheap clothes and toys that are sold all over the world. People live in flats, but there is still not enough room for everyone in the crowded city.

▶ **Thousands of Chinese people live on houseboats on the sea or tied together in Hong Kong harbour.**

◀ **Taiwanese farmers leave rice to dry on the roadside after it is harvested.**

Taiwan (say 'tie-wan') is a mountainous island in the South China Sea. Many people work on the land. Farmers grow rice, tea, pineapples and sugar cane. Factories make plastics, television sets, clothes and other products that are sold all around the world.

Japan and North and South Korea

Mountains and hills cover most of Japan's small islands. This leaves little room for its many people. Most Japanese live on the narrow strips of flat land around the coasts. Hot summers and mild winters are good for rice farming. Japan's cities are among the most important **manufacturing** centres in the world.

▶ Crowds fill the centre of Tokyo, Japan's busy capital city.

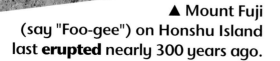

▲ Mount Fuji (say "Foo-gee") on Honshu Island last **erupted** nearly 300 years ago.

Farmers dig wide, flat steps into Japan's hillsides to make space for crops. But much of their food comes from the sea. Japanese eat about nine times as much fish as anyone else.

Japanese factories and offices use the most advanced **technology**. Robots make cameras, computers, cars and videos that are sold all over the world.

▼ Girl drummers take part in one of Japan's spectacular and colourful festivals.

Animals and plants

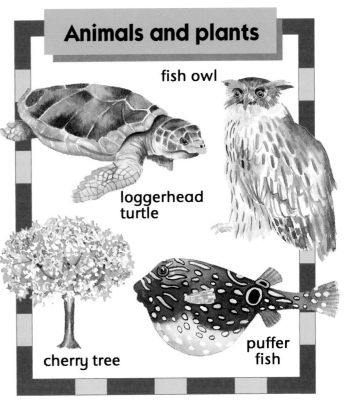

fish owl

loggerhead turtle

cherry tree

puffer fish

Tsunami and typhoons

The Japanese are used to the shaking and shuddering of **earthquakes**. When one occurs under the sea it makes a big wave called a tsunami (say "sue-nam-ee"), which batters the coast. Typhoons (say "tie-foons") are violent storms that usually hit Japan in the autumn.

Korea was divided into North and South Korea in 1945. Like Japan, forests and mountains cover much of the land. Farmers produce rice and silk, and factories make steel, clothes and other products.

▲ This pagoda, in South Korea, is a kind of temple. Each floor, or storey, has its own roof.

Southeast Asia

MYANMAR

South China Sea

Hanoi

LAOS

Manila

Vientiane

River Mekong

River Irrawaddy

VIETNAM

PHIL

THAILAND

CAMBODIA

Yangon

Bangkok

INDIAN OCEAN

Phnom Penh

BRUNEI

MALAYSIA

Kuala Lumpur

SINGAPORE

Borneo

Sumatra

IND

Southeast Asia is a hot, wet area of **volcanic islands** and **mainland** near the Equator. The country of Indonesia has more than thirteen thousand islands. Many other islands are separate countries. The land is mainly mountainous and covered with thick rainforest. Most people live and work in villages beside the rivers or along the coast.

Java

Jakarta

Bogor

76

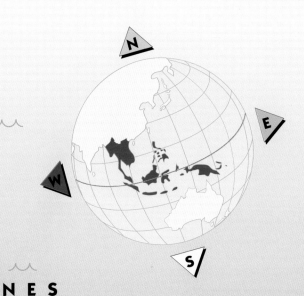

Did you know?

In Bogor, on Java, there is thunder almost every night of the year.

The rafflesia plant of Malaysia has the largest flower in the world. It can be almost one metre across and weigh as much as three newborn babies.

Akha women of Thailand (say 'tie-land') wear headdresses that are heavier than a big sack of potatoes.

Equator

...INES

PACIFIC OCEAN

PAPUA NEW GUINEA

New Guinea

★ Port Moresby

Sulawesi

...ESIA

EAST TIMOR

AUSTRALIA

Land on this map

rainforest

mountains

77

Southeast Asia

There are few roads in Southeast Asia. People travel by boat along the large rivers that flow through the rainforest. They build their villages in clearings on the riverbanks and along the coast. Their homes are often built on stilts. This keeps them dry when the rivers **flood** after heavy rain.

The rainforest is noisy with the calls of wild orang-utans, proboscis monkeys (say "pro-bos-kiss"), frogs, birds and insects. Trees are cut down to make space to grow rice and pineapples.

▲ These children live in the Philippines. Their house on stilts is built of bamboo.

Animals and plants

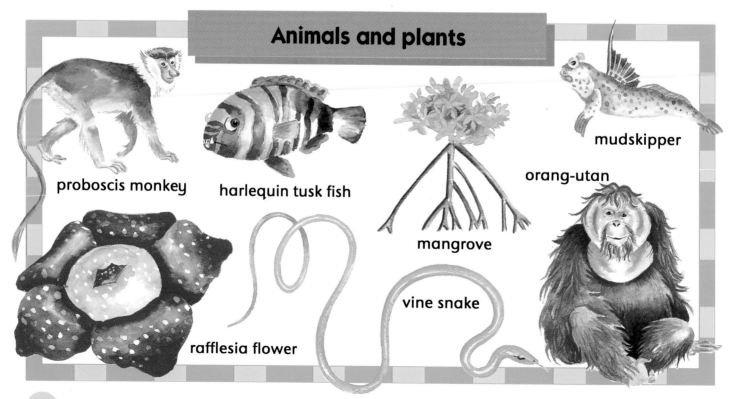

proboscis monkey

harlequin tusk fish

mangrove

mudskipper

orang-utan

vine snake

rafflesia flower

Singapore is one of the world's most important centres of business and banking, and the biggest port for ships travelling in Southeast Asia.

▶ In Java, women and children tap rubber from rubber trees. They cut deep grooves in the bark and let the rubber trickle down into cups underneath.

▼ Farmers in Thailand (say "Tie-land") bring fruit and vegetables by boat to sell in Bangkok's floating market.

Australia and New Zealand

Australia is the only country in the world that is also a continent, Australasia. It is just south of Southeast Asia. Europe and North America are on the opposite side of the world. This means that the time of day and the seasons are also opposite. When it is daytime in Australia, it is night-time in France. When it is spring in New Zealand, it is autumn in the United Kingdom.

INDIAN OCEAN

• Darwin

Northern Territory

AUSTRALIA

Alice Springs •

Uluru (Ayers Rock)

Gibson Desert

Great Victoria Desert

South Australia

Western Australia

Lak Eyr

• Perth

Adelaid

Did you know?

South Australia's Lake Eyre is the only lake that isn't a lake. Most of the time it is covered by a crust of salt nearly four metres thick.

The underwater Great Barrier Reef is the world's largest structure built by living things.

Uluru is the largest single rock in the world. It is two and a half kilometres long and 300 metres high.

N

W   E

S

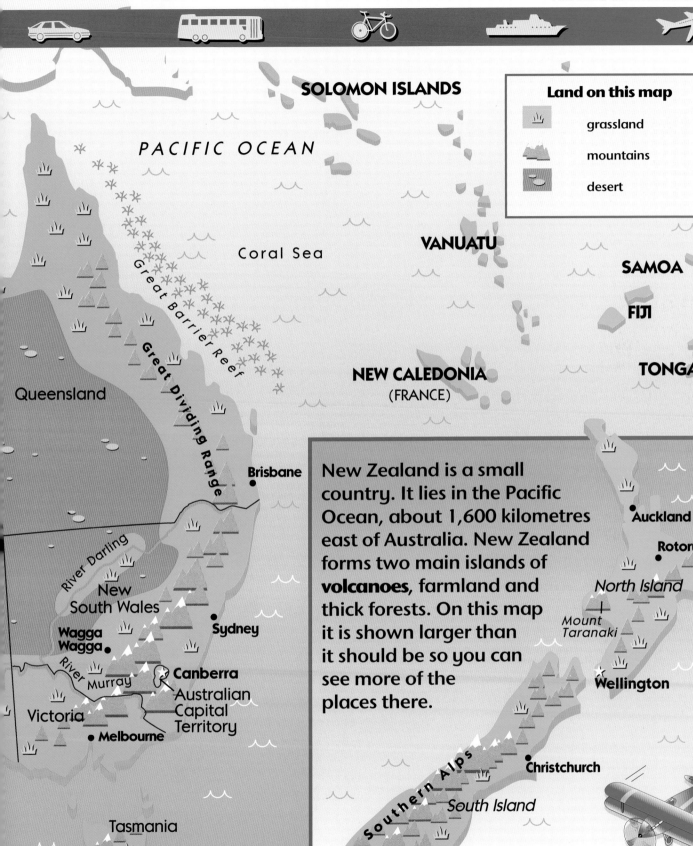

SOLOMON ISLANDS

PACIFIC OCEAN

Coral Sea

VANUATU

SAMOA

FIJI

Land on this map

grassland

mountains

desert

NEW CALEDONIA
(FRANCE)

TONGA

Queensland

Great Barrier Reef

Great Dividing Range

● Brisbane

River Darling

New South Wales

● Sydney

Wagga Wagga ●

River Murray

● **Canberra**

Australian Capital Territory

Victoria

● **Melbourne**

Tasmania

● **Hobart**

New Zealand is a small country. It lies in the Pacific Ocean, about 1,600 kilometres east of Australia. New Zealand forms two main islands of **volcanoes**, farmland and thick forests. On this map it is shown larger than it should be so you can see more of the places there.

● **Auckland**

● **Rotorua**

North Island

Mount Taranaki

★ **Wellington**

Southern Alps

● **Christchurch**

South Island

NEW ZEALAND

Stewart Island

Australia

▼ Aboriginal Australians believe Uluru is a magical place.

Australia is made up of six **states**, including the island state of Tasmania, and two **territories**. Its land is mostly dry, hot desert and bush country called outback. **Iron ore** colours the soil rust-red. Most people live in cities, such as Sydney and Perth, close to the coasts of southeast and southwest Australia, where it is cooler and the land is good for farming.

▲ These girls are college students in Alice Springs.

Native Australians are called Aboriginal Australians, (say 'ab-o-ridge-in-al'). They were here for fifty thousand years before European settlers arrived. Most Aboriginal Australians live in towns and cities, but some still live in the outback. Many towns and settlements have Aboriginal names, such as Wagga Wagga.

Australia is one of the world's biggest producers of wool and beef. Families who live on cattle stations in the outback may be hundreds of kilometres from their nearest neighbours. Workers called jackaroos round up the cattle by plane, lorry and on horseback.

The famous Great Barrier Reef lies off Australia's northeast coast. It is made of **coral**, which is the hardened **skeletons** of tiny sea creatures called polyps, (say "pol-ips"). Millions of living coral polyps are attached to the reef.

▼ Bright, tropical fish swim among 300 types of coral on the Great Barrier Reef.

Animals and plants

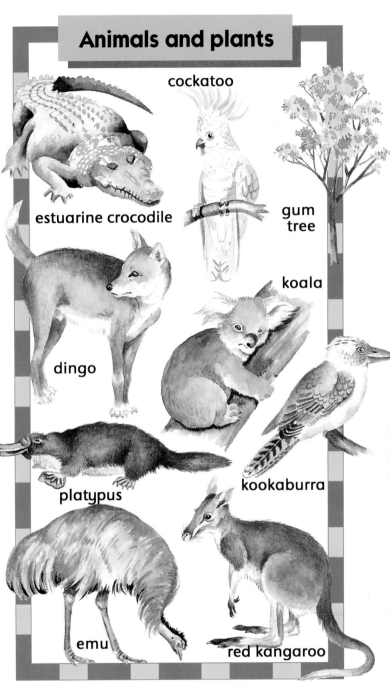

cockatoo

estuarine crocodile

gum tree

koala

dingo

platypus

kookaburra

emu

red kangaroo

There are many unusual animals that live only in Australia, such as the koala and platypus. The most common of these animals is the big, grey kangaroo which can be seen in parks and in bush country.

New Zealand

Maori (say "Mauw-ree") were the first people to live in New Zealand. They arrived more than 1,000 years ago. They came in canoes from other faraway Pacific islands. People from Europe started to come here about 200 years ago. Today about three-quarters of New Zealanders are **descendants** of those Europeans.

► This farmhouse, built of wood, is at the foot of Mount Taranaki, one of North Island's many **volcanoes**.

▼ Children in New Zealand play old Maori games.

84

Many New Zealanders live and work on fruit or sheep farms. New Zealand is the world's biggest producer of lamb. It is also home for several unusual wild animals that are found only in New Zealand's islands. The kiwi, the takahe, the kakapo and the tuatara lizard are examples.

Animals and plants

tuatara

weta

pohutukawa

punga

takahe

kakapo

kiwi

Geysers and hot springs

Near Rotorua, the Earth's crust is so thin that steam from hot underground streams sizzles like a boiling kettle out of cracks in the ground.

▲ A **geyser** is a jet of hot water that escapes from underground like steam from a kettle. This geyser is near Rotorua in North Island.

Antarctica

Antarctica is the highest, stormiest, coldest and most southerly continent in the world. Every direction is north from here. It is just south of the Antarctic Circle. The South Pole is at its centre. The ice that covers it is nearly five kilometres thick in some places. It never melts. Antarctica is bigger than Europe, but it has no native people. Scientists, tourists, fish and birds are its only visitors.

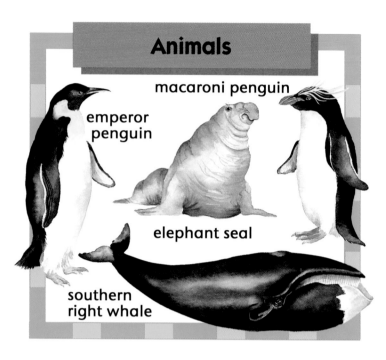

Animals

macaroni penguin

emperor penguin

elephant seal

southern right whale

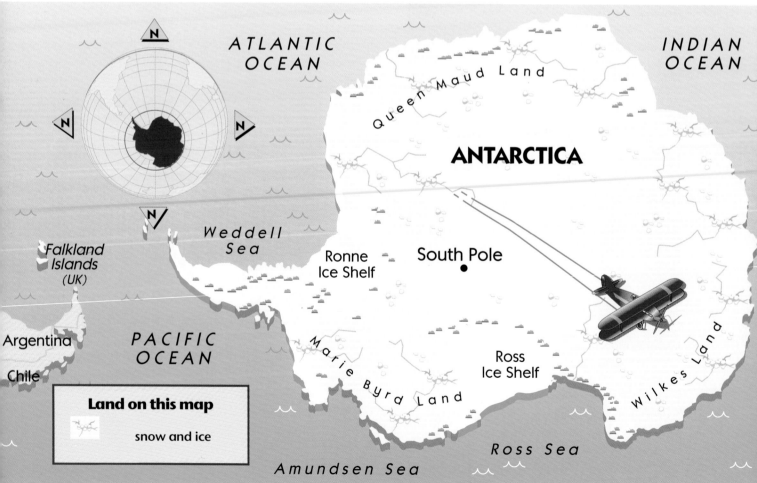

N

ATLANTIC OCEAN

INDIAN OCEAN

Queen Maud Land

ANTARCTICA

N

N

N

Weddell Sea

Falkland Islands (UK)

Ronne Ice Shelf

South Pole

Argentina

PACIFIC OCEAN

Chile

Marie Byrd Land

Ross Ice Shelf

Wilkes Land

Land on this map

snow and ice

Ross Sea

Amundsen Sea

No country owns Antarctica but several nations have built permanent **research stations** here. Some countries would like to explore for minerals, such as gold and silver. Others want Antarctica to be protected as a world park. They have to take important decisions together to control what happens.

Glossary

Ancestors The members of your family who lived and died many years ago.

Canyon A narrow, rocky **valley** with steep sides.

Civilization A well-organized country or large group of people. Most civilizations have big cities, schools, hospitals and museums.

Climate The sort of weather that is usual in a particular area or country.

Communism A set of ideas about the way a country should be run. The main idea is that all people should share all their money equally. In most communist countries, the government controls schools, farms, hospitals and factories.

Compressed Something that is very tightly squeezed or squashed.

Coral A hard substance found under the sea. It is made from the **skeletons** of millions of tiny animals called polyps.

Descendants Your children and your children's children. You are descended from your parents and grandparents.

Earthquake When a piece of the Earth's crust grinds against another piece, the ground trembles and cracks open.

Erupt The explosion of hot gas and rock inside a **volcano**.

Fertile Land that has soil which is good for growing healthy crops.

Flood A large amount of water covering an area that is usually dry. It is normally caused by very heavy rains.

Geyser Jets of hot water that escape from hot underground rock.

Glacier A river of ice that moves slowly down a mountainside. They are found mainly in very cold lands around the North and South Pole.

Globe An object shaped like a ball with a map of the Earth on it.

Gourd A large fruit with a tough skin. Empty gourds are often used to make large containers for carrying water and food.

Illegal Something that is against the law.

Independent country A country or countries that have their own governments and make their own laws.

Industry The work that goes into making goods in factories. Industrial describes something that makes goods, such as an industrial town or machinery.

Irrigate To supply dry farmland with water.

Iron ore A strong, hard metal found in rocks and earth.

Landmark A particular feature in a landscape, such as a hill or a mountain.

Mainland The main part of a country that does not include any islands that lie off the coast.

Manufacture If you manufacture something, you make it. Things such as cars and washing machines are manufactured.

Navigable A river or lake that is wide enough and deep enough to sail a boat on.

Nomad A person who does not live in a fixed place. Nomadic people often take their animals, such as cattle, with them as they move around looking for food.

Oasis (oases) A place in the desert where water bubbles up to the surface from underground streams.

Plain A large, flat area of land with very few trees. In some countries, plains are also called prairies, steppes or pampas.

Poacher A person who hunts animals that are living on protected or private land.

Region A particular area of land, such as the Arctic region around the North Pole.

Religion The belief in a god or gods.

Research station A place where scientists can study the animals, plants, minerals, landscape, weather or people in an area.

Retire When older people retire they no longer have to go to work.

Sand dune A hill or mound made from sand.

Sandstone A type of rock made from sand. It is often used to make bricks for buildings.

Skeleton The bony frame that protects and holds up the body of an animal.

State A particular area of some large countries such as the United States and Australia.

Symbol A code that stands for a real object. The symbol may be a shape or a small picture. For example, a picture of a tree is a symbol for a real forest on the maps in this encyclopedia.

Technology The study of machines and how they are used.

Temperature How hot or cold something is.

Territory An area of land that is separate from but belongs to a country.

Textiles Woven clothes or fabrics.

Valley A stretch of land that lies in between hills, often with a river flowing through it.

Volcanic island An island that is formed by the **eruption** of **volcanoes** beneath the ocean. Liquid rock emptying from the volcano forms layers which eventually rise above the ocean surface.

Volcano An opening in the Earth's surface where gases and very hot liquid rock escape. Volcanoes are found in mountain chains on land and under the sea.

Index

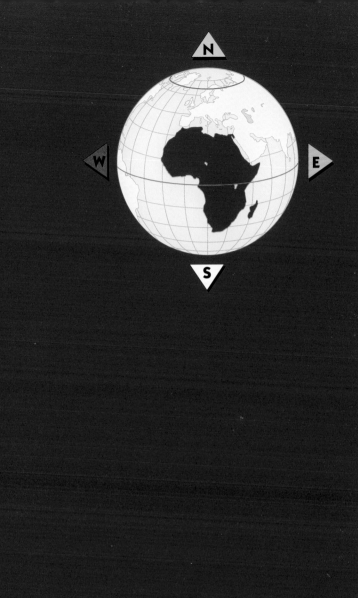